D1787614

QUOTATIONS FROM

AFRICAN AMERICANS

TO _____

FROM _____

DATE _____

I DREAM A WORLD

I DREAM A WORLD WHERE MAN
NO OTHER WILL SCORN,
WHERE LOVE WILL BLESS THE EARTH
AND PEACE ITS PATHS ADORN.
I DREAM A WORLD WHERE ALL
WILL KNOW SWEET FREEDOM'S WAY,
WHERE GREED NO LONGER
SAPS THE SOUL
NOR AVARICE BLIGHTS OUR DAY.
A WORLD I DREAM WHERE
BLACK OR WHITE,
WHATEVER RACE YOU BE,
WILL SHARE THE BOUNTIES OF THE EARTH
AND EVERY MAN IS FREE
WHERE WRETCHEDNESS WILL
HANG ITS HEAD
AND JOY, LIKE A PEARL,
ATTEND THE NEEDS OF ALL MANKIND.
OF SUCH I DREAM -
OUR WORLD !

Langston Hughes

AMERICA IS ME.

IT GAVE ME THE ONLY LIFE

I KNOW

SO I MUST SHARE

IN ITS SURVIVAL.

Gordon Parks

WHEN A MAN

ANGERS YOU,

HE CONQUERS YOU.

Toni Morrison

BE AS YOU ARE

AND HOPE

THAT IT'S RIGHT.

Dizzy Gillespie

FIND THE GOOD.

IT'S ALL AROUND YOU.

FIND IT, SHOWCASE IT AND

YOU'LL START

BELIEVING IN IT.

Jesse Owens

THEM THAT'S GOT,

SHALL GET.

THEM THAT'S NOT,

SHALL LOVE.

SO THE BIBLE SAID.

AND IT STILL IS NEWS.

MAMA MAY HAVE.

PAPA MAY HAVE.

BUT GOD BLESS THE CHILD.

THAT'S GOT HIS OWN.

Billie Holiday

It's a business where everybody puts so many daggers in your back, you look like a porcupine.

Don King

THERE IS NEVER TIME

IN THE FUTURE IN WHICH

WE WILL WORK OUT

OUR SALVATION.

THE CHALLENGE IS IN

THE MOMENT, THE TIME

IS ALWAYS NOW.

James Baldwin

THE GREAT CHALLENGE IS
TO PREPARE OURSELVES TO
ENTER THESE
DOORS OF OPPORTUNITY.

Martin Luther King, Jr.

IGNORANCE, ARROGANCE,

AND RACISM HAVE

BLOOMED AS SUPERIOR

KNOWLEDGE IN ALL

TOO MANY UNIVERSITIES.

Alice Walker

I WON'T HAVE ANY MONEY

TO LEAVE BEHIND.

I WON'T HAVE THE FINE

AND LUXURIOUS THINGS OF

LIFE TO LEAVE BEHIND.

BUT I JUST WANT TO LEAVE

A COMMITTED LIFE BEHIND.

Martin Luther King, Jr.

WHATEVER I'M DOING,
I DON'T THINK IN TERMS
OF TOMORROW.

Anita Baker

In order to have a

conversation with

someone, you must

reveal yourself.

James Baldwin

He who is not

courageous enough

to take risks will

accomplish nothing

in life.

Muhammad Ali

WHEN WE DIE,

IT'S SURE ENOUGH FOR

THE FIRST TIME.

I'LL BE INTERESTED TO SEE

HOW IT COMES OUT,

BUT I'M IN NO HURRY.

Ray Charles

I'M BLACK.

I DON'T FEEL BURDENED

BY IT AND I DON'T THINK

IT'S A HUGE RESPONSIBILITY.

IT'S PART OF WHO I AM.

IT DOES NOT DEFINE ME.

Oprah Winfrey

YOU CAN'T JUST SIT THERE

AND WAIT FOR PEOPLE

TO GIVE YOU THAT GOLDEN

DREAM, YOU'VE GOT TO GET

OUT THERE AND MAKE IT

HAPPEN FOR YOURSELF.

Diana Ross

I TRY TO DO THE RIGHT
THING AT THE RIGHT TIME.
THEY MAY JUST BE
LITTLE THINGS, BUT
USUALLY THEY MAKE
THE DIFFERENCE BETWEEN
WINNING AND LOSING.

Kareem Abdul Jabbar

WE ARE NOT

MAKERS OF HISTORY.

WE ARE

MADE BY HISTORY.

Martin Luther King, Jr.

I AM NEITHER A
FANATIC NOR A DREAMER.
I AM A BLACK MAN
WHO LOVES PEACE AND
JUSTICE AND LOVES
HIS PEOPLE.

Malcolm X

Ten or fifteen years

ago, you could tell

the brothers from

the cousins.

Not anymore.

Everybody (sounds)

Black - except

John Denver.

Sammy Davis, Jr

Experience, which

DESTROYS INNOCENCE,

ALSO LEADS ONE

BACK TO IT.

James Baldwin

WE ALL DO

"DO, RE, MI,"

BUT YOU HAVE GOT TO

FIND THE OTHER

NOTES YOURSELF.

Louis Armstrong

FEW ARE TOO YOUNG,

AND NONE TOO OLD,

TO MAKE THE

ATTEMPT TO LEARN.

Booker T. Washington

I'M TOO YOUNG

TO BE A LEGEND.

I'M STILL THE LADY

NEXT DOOR.

THAT KEEPS MY FEET

ON THE GROUND.

Aretha Franklin

HOW FAR YOU GO IN LIFE
DEPENDS ON YOUR BEING
TENDER WITH THE YOUNG,
COMPASSIONATE WITH THE
AGED, SYMPATHETIC WITH
THE STRIVING, AND
TOLERANT OF THE WEAK AND
STRONG. BECAUSE SOMEDAY
IN LIFE YOU WILL HAVE BEEN
ALL OF THESE.

George Washington Carver

THIS LIFE IS NOT REAL.

I CONQUERED THE WORLD

AND IT DID NOT

BRING ME SATISFACTION.

Muhammad Ali

To LIVE IS TO SUFFER;

TO SURVIVE IS TO

FIND SOME MEANING

IN THE SUFFERING.

Roberta Flack

LIGHT HAS COME

INTO THE WORLD,

AND EVERY MAN MUST

DECIDE WHETHER HE WILL

WALK IN THE LIGHT

OF CREATIVE ALTRUISM

OR THE DARKNESS OF

DESTRUCTIVE SELFISHNESS.

Martin Luther King, Jr.

LOVE DOES NOT BEGIN

AND END THE WAY WE

SEEM TO THINK IT DOES.

LOVE IS A BATTLE,

LOVE IS A WAR,

LOVE IS GROWING UP.

James Baldwin

I HEAR THAT POT STUFF

A LOT, ALL I CAN SAY IS

WE HAVEN'T MELTED YET.

Jesse Jackson

I'M MOTIVATED.

THE SPIRIT HITS ME

AND I JUST KEEP GOING

AND DON'T STOP.

THE MORE I PLAY,

THE MORE I CAN INVENT,

THE MORE IDEAS

COME TO ME.

Lionel Hampton

YOU ARE THE PRODUCT

OF THE LOVE AND AFFECTION

OF YOUR PARENTS, AND

THROUGHOUT YOUR LIFE

YOU HAVE DRAWN

STRENGTH AND HOPE FROM

THAT LOVE AND SECURITY.

Nelson Mandela

I DANCED,

I PAID THE PIPER AND

LEFT HIM A BIG FAT TIP.

Joe Louis

OUR FAMILY

WAS SO POOR

WE WOULD EAT

THE HOLE OUT OF

A DOUGHNUT.

Malcolm X

THERE IS NOTHING ESSENTIALLY WRONG WITH POWER. THE PROBLEM IS AMERICAN POWER IS UNEQUALLY DISTRIBUTED.

Martin Luther King, Jr.

Of my two "handicaps,"

being female put

many more obstacles

in my path than

being Black.

Shirley Chisholm

BUT FOR OURSELVES

WHO KNOW OUR PLIGHT

TOO WELL, THERE IS A

NEED OF GREAT PATTERNS

TO GUIDE US, GREAT

LIVES...TO INSPIRE US,

STRONG MEN AND WOMEN

TO LIFT US UP AND GIVE US

CONFIDENCE IN THE

POWERS WE, TOO, POSSESS.

Langston Hughes

Every intersection

in the road of life

is an opportunity

to make a decision,

and at some time

to only listen.

Duke Ellington

We've just got to let
them know that we
know what they are
doing and that we're
not going to lighten up
until they stop.

Miles Davis

INSTEAD OF ALWAYS
LOOKING AT THE PAST,
I PUT MYSELF AHEAD
TWENTY YEARS AND TRY
TO LOOK AT WHAT I NEED
TO DO NOW IN ORDER
TO GET THERE THEN.

Diana Ross

RACISM IS A CONTEMPT
FOR LIFE, AN ARROGANT
ASSERTION THAT ONE RACE
IS THE CENTER OF VALUE
AND OBJECT OF DEVOTION,
BEFORE WHICH OTHER RACES
MUST KNEEL IN SUBMISSION.

Martin Luther King, Jr.

RECOGNITION WILL DO

MORE TO CEMENT THE

FRIENDSHIP OF RACES

THAN ANY OCCURRENCE

SINCE THE DAWN

OF FREEDOM.

Booker T. Washington

WE ARE RESPONSIBLE

FOR THE WORLD IN WHICH

WE FIND OURSELVES,

IF ONLY BECAUSE WE ARE

THE ONLY SENTIENT FORCE

WHICH CAN CHANGE IT.

James Baldwin

EVERYTHING THAT WE

SEE IS A SHADOW CAST

BY THAT WHICH WE

DO NOT SEE.

Martin Luther King, Jr.

Soul is like electricity -

we don't know what it is,

but it's a force

that can light a room.

Ray Charles

Don't let people

put labels on you - and

don't put them

on yourself.

Sometimes a label

can kill you.

Malcolm X

FRIENDS ARE MY HEART

AND MY EARS.

Michael Jordan

To be successful,

grow to the point

where one completely

forgets himself;

that is, to lose himself

in a great cause.

Booker T. Washington

ANYTIME YOU SEE
SOMEONE MORE SUCCESSFUL
THAN YOU ARE,
THEY ARE DOING SOMETHING
THAT YOU AREN'T.

Malcolm X

Success is the result of perfection, hard work, learning from failure, loyalty, and persistence.

Colin Powell

I THINK IT PISSES GOD OFF

IF YOU WALK BY THE

COLOR PURPLE IN

A FIELD SOMEWHERE AND

DON'T NOTICE IT.

Alice Walker

THE MOST POTENT

WEAPON IN THE HANDS

OF THE OPPRESSOR IS THE

MIND OF THE OPPRESSED.

Steven Biko

SAY IT LOUD: "I'M BLACK AND I'M PROUD."

James Brown

IF A MAN HASN'T

DISCOVERED SOMETHING

THAT HE WILL DIE FOR,

HE ISN'T FIT TO LIVE.

Martin Luther King, Jr.

MAN MUST EVOLVE

FOR ALL HUMAN CONFLICT

A METHOD WHICH REJECTS

REVENGE, AGGRESSION,

AND RETALIATION.

THE FOUNDATION OF SUCH

A METHOD IS LOVE.

Martin Luther King, Jr.

ONE CAN ONLY FACE

IN OTHERS WHAT ONE CAN

FACE IN ONESELF.

James Baldwin

I BEG OF YOU TO STUDY.
YOUR KNOWLEDGE, YOUR
EDUCATION IS YOUR
HUSBAND. YOUR HUSBAND
MAY LEAVE YOU, BUT WHAT
YOU HAVE IN YOUR MIND
WILL NEVER LEAVE YOU.

Miriam Makeba

HE WHO STARTS IN

THE RACE MUST FOREVER

REMAIN BEHIND OR

RUN FASTER THAN

THE MAN IN FRONT.

Martin Luther King, Jr.

LIFE IS LIKE A BUTTERFLY.

YOU CAN CHASE IT,

OR YOU CAN LET IT

COME TO YOU.

Ruth Brown

LIFE IS FINDING

DIFFERENT TASKMASTERS.

Marvin Gaye

Let our opportunities

overshadow our

grievances.

Booker T. Washington

WE MUST PAY OUR

DEBTS TO THE PAST

BY PUTTING THE FUTURE

IN DEBT TO OURSELVES.

Alice Walker

$\mathbf{Y}$OU HAVE TO EXPECT

THINGS OF YOURSELF

BEFORE YOU CAN DO THEM.

Michael Jordan

YOU LEAVE HOME TO

SEEK YOUR FORTUNE

AND WHEN YOU GET IT,

YOU GO HOME AND SHARE IT

WITH YOUR FAMILY.

Anita Baker

LET NOTHING AND NOBODY

BREAK YOUR SPIRIT.

LET THE UNITY

IN THE COMMUNITY

REMAIN INTACT.

Jesse Jackson

W E ARE ONE,

OUR CAUSE IS ONE,

AND WE MUST

HELP EACH OTHER;

IF WE ARE TO SUCCEED.

Frederick Douglass

IF YOU UNDERSTOOD

EVERYTHING I SAY,

YOU'D BE ME.

Miles Davis

WHEN FACE TO FACE
WITH ONESELF OR LOOKING
ONESELF IN THE EYE,
THERE IS NO COP OUT.
IT IS THE MOMENT
OF TRUTH. I CANNOT
LIE TO ME.

Duke Ellington

Nations, like men,

are wary of truth,

for truth is too often

not beautiful.

Addison Gayle, Jr.

BECAUSE TIME HAS BEEN

GOOD TO ME,

I TREAT IT WITH

GREAT RESPECT.

Lena Horne

WHEN ONE IS TOO OLD

FOR LOVE, ONE FINDS

GREAT COMFORT

IN GOOD DINNERS.

Zora Neale Hurston

GIVE YOUR BRAIN

AS MUCH ATTENTION

AS YOU DO YOUR HAIR

AND YOU'LL BE A THOUSAND

TIMES BETTER OFF.

Malcolm X

BE AS YOU ARE

AND HOPE

THAT IT'S RIGHT.

Dizzy Gillespie

I'VE OUTDONE ANYONE
YOU CAN NAME - MOZART,
BEETHOVEN, BACH,
STRAUSS.
IRVING BERLIN, HE WROTE
1,001 TUNES.
I WROTE 5,500.

James Brown

SOMETIMES

I AMAZE MYSELF.

I SAY THIS HUMBLY.

Don King

I WAS A DRUM MAJOR

FOR JUSTICE.

Martin Luther King, Jr.

I BELIEVE IN HUMAN RIGHTS FOR EVERYONE, AND NONE OF US IS QUALIFIED TO JUDGE EACH OTHER AND THAT NONE OF US SHOULD THEREFORE HAVE THAT AUTHORITY.

Malcolm X

Other Titles by Great Quotations Publishing Company
COMB BOUND

A Friend Is

A Smile Increases Your Face Value

Aged to Perfection

An Apple A Day

Backfield in Motion

Batter Up

Bedside Manner

Believe and Achieve

Best in Business Humor

Birthday Wishes

Books Are Better

Boyfriends Live Longer Than Husbands

Change Your Thoughts,
    Change Your Life

Don't Marry, Be Happy

Double Dribble

Golf Humor

Graduation - Keys To Success

Great Quotes - Great Comedians

Halfway Home (Surviving
    the Middle Years)

Harvest Of THoughts

Inspirations

Joy Of Family

Keys To Happiness

Life's Winning Tips

Love, Honor, Cherish

Love, Sex & Marriage

Love On Your Wedding Day

Mothers And Babies

Never Give Up

Our Life Together

Over The Hill Sex

Political Humor

Quotations from African-American

Real Friends

Retirement

Sports Poop

Sports Quotes

Stress

Teachers Inspirations

Thank You

The Quest For Success

Things You'll Learn

Thinking Of You

Thoughts From The Heart

To A Very Special Daughter

To A Very Special Son

To A Very Special Grandparent

To A Very Special Love

To My Mother

To My Father

Unofficial Christmas Survival Guide

Unofficial Executive Survival Guide

Unofficial Stress Test

Unofficial Survival Guide
    to Parenthood

Unofficial Vacation Guide

Ordinary Men, Extraordinary Lives

Our Thoughts Are Prayors

What To Tell Your Children

Who Really Said

Wonders & Joys Of Christmas

Words From Great Women

PAPERBACK

199 Useful Things to Do With
  A Politician
201 Best Things Ever Said
A Lifetime of Love
A Light Heart Lives Long
A Teacher Is Better Than Two Books
As A Cat Thinketh
Cheatnotes On Life
Chicken Soup
Dear Mr. President
Father Knows Best
Food For Thought
Golden Years/Golden Words
Happiness Walks On Busy Feet
Heal The World
Hooked on Golf
Hollywords
I'm Not Over The Hill

In Celebration of Women
Life's Simple Pleasures
Mother - A Bouquet of Love
Motivation Magic
Mrs. Webster's Dictionary
Reflections
Romantic Rendezvous
Sports Page
So Many Ways To Say
  Thank You
The ABC's of Parenting
The Best Of Friends
The Birthday Astrologer
The Little Book of
  Spiritual Wisdom
Things You'll Learn,
  If You Live Long Enough

PERPETUAL CALENDARS

Apple A Day
Country Proverbs
Each Day A New Beginning
Friends Forever
Golf Forever
Home Is Where The Heart Is
Proverbs
Seasonings
Simply The Best Dad
Simple The Best Mom
Simple Ways To Say I Love You
Teacher"s" Are "First Class!"

Great Quotations Publishing Company
1967 Quincy Court
Glendale Heights, IL 60139-2045
Phone (708) 582-2800
FAX (708) 582-2813